Beauty Matters

Creating a High Aesthetic in School Culture

Stephen R. Turley, Ph.D.

TURLEY TALKS

A New Conservative Age is Rising
www.TurleyTalks.com

Table of Contents

INTRODUCTION

This book is about understanding Beauty and appreciating how Beauty affects the loves of our students. My concern here is that as parents and educators in the classical school movement, our efforts in teaching the True, the Good, and the Beautiful tend to put an emphasis on the first two at the expense of the third. We are generally competent with Truth, especially in view of the emphasis on the importance of forming the worldview of a student. And we are relatively proficient with Goodness in terms of the moral dimension of our faith and how it pertains to classroom discipline and the like. But when it comes to Beauty, what it is and how we teach it, our certainties dissipate, and all kinds of confusion take over.

For example, in my own teaching experience at both the high school and university levels, I have seen firsthand how modernist assumptions have worked themselves out in the lives of our students. When I call students at both the classical school and the university at which I teach to give a basic account for the classical conception of Beauty, the answers to my inquiries consistently exemplify a complete and total devotion to aesthetic relativism. I am not exaggerating in the least. In fact, if you query among your own teachers and parents as to whether there is such a thing as objective Beauty and, if so, what is it, how do you identify it, what is its function and role in the life of the student and the school, I don't think the answers forthcoming will impress you.

This suggests to me that while we have put much thought into teaching Truth and Goodness in our classical schools, we have done so at the expense of teaching Beauty, and I ought to confess: I'm not immune from this! I've taught Apologetics for years alongside a course in Aesthetics, and I never even noticed the absence of the latter in the former. For example, when I teach the basic elements of a worldview in Apologetics, I focus on five constituents: theology, metaphysics, anthropology, epistemology, and ethics. But notice what's missing: no aesthetics! Our worldviews are comprised of Truth and Goodness ... but no Beauty!

I am very concerned that our educational efforts are in fact being undermined by a ubiquitously present relativism coming in through the back door. Truth, Goodness, and Beauty are not sequestered from one another – they need each other and they imply one another. And if Beauty is robbed of its transcendent nature and relocated solely within the private psychological processes, then Truth and Goodness are sure to follow.

But what I've found is that when students really do encounter Beauty, guess what? They find it beautiful! They're enamored by it, they love it; they are attracted to Beauty, as is entailed in the concept itself. I'm repeatedly told by my students when they're seniors that their favorite class of mine was Aesthetics, the study and encounter of Beauty. Growing up, they always felt that something critical was missing from their education and worldview training, and when they find Beauty, they recognize: "That's it! That's what's been missing!"

In what follows, I want to offer you a primer of sorts on Beauty. We will first explore what Beauty is, particularly in relation to Truth and Goodness. We will then explore the relation of Beauty to the formation of virtue in the lives of our students. We shall then discover some representative ways for beautifying our schools and transforming them into sacred spaces for the contemplation of the True, the Good, and the Beautiful.

PART I

BEAUTY MATTERS

CHAPTER 1

What is Beauty?

To understand Beauty, we have to see its relationship to Truth and Goodness. The three terms are well used in our classical Christian education parlance, but it would be good here to start with an overview of what these terms actually mean.

The terms Truth, Goodness, and Beauty (Greek: *alēthia, agathos*, and *kalos*) featured relatively prominently in Greek life by the time of Plato (c. 428-347 BC). In the fifth-century BC, the upstanding citizens of the polis, the Greek city-state, were designated as the *kalos kai agathos,* the "beautiful and the good," a designation that was later contracted into a single term, *kalokagathia.*

But it is not until Plato that you get this systematic interplay between Truth, Goodness, and Beauty as macrocosmic values on the one hand, and the human soul as a sort of microcosmic replication of those values on the other. Because human beings are created in the image of Truth, Goodness, and Beauty, as it were, we also have a three-fold dimensionality to our souls: the intellectual, moral, and emotional, made popular by Aristotle's three modes of rhetorical persuasion: *logos*, *ethos*, and *pathos*. This interplay between the

macrocosmic values of Truth, Goodness, and Beauty on the one hand and the threefold capacities of the microcosmic soul of intellect, ethic, and emotion on the other, will be very important in understanding the role of Beauty in the formation of virtue in the lives of our students.

However, let's make sure we have a firm grasp on what each term means:

The Greek term *alēthia* (Truth) literally means "to reveal or disclose." It is a negation of the word, *lethein*, which means "to conceal"; truth reveals the nature of reality to our intellectual capacities, our *logos*.

The term *agathos* (Goodness) connotes "the excellence of a thing or person," and was eventually developed by philosophers to designate the goal, purpose, or meaning of existence. My wife and I have a good marriage if we are fulfilling the purpose of marriage; I have a good watch if it tells time accurately. As Truth reveals reality to my intellectual capacities, Goodness reveals reality to my volitional and moral capacities, what Aristotle termed *ethos* or Plato, *thymos.*

But what is perhaps most stunning in this micro-macrocosmic relationship is the role Plato ascribes to *kalos* or Beauty, particularly in Diotima's speech in his work entitled *The Symposium*. For Plato and virtually all subsequent classical and Christian philosophers and theologians, Beauty is the loveliness, the radiance, the delightfulness, the delectableness of the True and the Good, that draws the human person toward Truth and Goodness by directing what Plato called our *eros* (Aristotle's *pathos*) or a loving desire within the human person.

It is crucial to note here that Beauty is a physics in the classical world. This is why we associate Beauty with *attraction*; Beauty is a gravitational pull, a tractor beam (for you *Star Wars* fans!). Through Beauty we are drawn to the True and the Good, the divine source of life, by the awakening of our desires. We desire whatever we find beautiful.

This is the first thing we want to make sure we've got nailed down; *Beauty is a physics*. Beauty is emphatically not a sentiment, or a personal preference; it's not a subjective opinion or inclination. In the classical world, Beauty functions like the law of attraction; it's a gravitational pull that exists outside of me and draws me somewhere, and by definition of the Beautiful – as radiance and delightfulness – it must draw me to the True and the Good.

But wait a minute! A moment's reflection will reveal that not everything I find Beautiful is True and Good. How can we say that Beauty by definition leads me to the True and the Good when I am often attracted to things that are emphatically not True and Good? Moreover, doesn't this discrepancy reveal a thoroughly personal dimension to Beauty? If you and I are attracted to different things, does that not mean that the Beautiful involves at least some degree of subjective sentiment and personal preference?

I mentioned above that the interplay between the macrocosmic values and the microcosmic soul will be very important in understanding the role of Beauty in the formation of virtue in the lives of our students. Such questions as these lead us precisely to such an interplay. In our next chapter, we will explore the role of Beauty in ordering our subjective loves.

CHAPTER 2

Beauty and Virtue: The Ordering of Our Loves

As classical educators dedicated to the teaching of the True, the Good, and the Beautiful, we have a major roadblock in front of us. The classical and Christian age believed that the world was filled with divine meaning and purpose, the cosmic values of Truth, Goodness, and Beauty, and the goal of education was to align the student's affections, desires, and loves with those cosmic values, so that they love what's truly lovely and desire what's truly desirable and hence experience human flourishing. Because of its devotion to scientific rationalism, our modern secular age does not believe the world is filled with divine meaning and purpose; instead, the world operates solely by biological, chemical, and physical causal laws. That's the True, the Good, and the Beautiful of the modern age: biology, chemistry, and physics which are considered value-neutral. Thus, there are no longer any cosmic values by which the student's affections can be rightly ordered and arranged. And so what we value, what we desire and love, is rendered completely subjective and person relative.

This is what our students are breathing in when they come in to the classroom and say: Who are you to define art? Who are you to say what's good music and what's bad music?

To counter that kind of secular skepticism, we have to offer our students a fundamentally different world, one that's filled with divine meaning and purpose and therefore obligates us to conform our lives into a harmonious relationship with it. Here's how C.S. Lewis put it in his *Abolition of Man*: "Until quite modern times, all teachers and even all men believed the universe to be such that certain emotional reactions on our part could be either congruous or incongruous to it— believed, in fact, that objects did not merely receive, but could *merit*, our approval or disapproval, our reverence, or our contempt."

He then summons some of history's greatest minds as witnesses to such a view of the world. He cites Augustine's conception of virtue as *ordo amoris,* the right ordering of our loves. We learn in Genesis that God has created a world that is good; every time God creates something, he ascribes to that thing an objective value or goodness, and that goodness has an order to it; in other words, while all things are good as God created them, he created an economy or order to that goodness. You will notice in Genesis that when God creates mankind, it's the first time he said, "And it was *very* good." Notice the superlative: all things in creation are good, but humanity is very good.

Now what Lewis is pointing out is that this orderly goodness in the world provides an objective model by which we are able to order our affections, since it is a world that merits our praise. So, for example, it is good to love a baby, and it is good to love a ham sandwich; but if both the baby and ham sandwich were falling off a ledge and I rush to save the ham sandwich, that's a bad; something has gone wrong with my loves. The order of my loves has been dislodged from the economy of goods that God has created.

We can see this affectional disordering in the Fall narrative of Genesis 3. Notice the ways in which Eve's inclinations are described: "When the woman saw that the tree was *good* for food, and that it was a *delight* to the eyes, and that the tree was *desirable* to make one wise..." (Gen 3:6). Note the emphasis on her desires and the affections; Eve was *attracted* to the fruit; the Fall came about through disordered loves, affections and inclinations dislodged from God's economy of goods. Hence, what is the greatest commandment? "Thou shalt love the Lord thy God with all thy heart, and with all thy soul, and with all thy mind. This is the first and great commandment. And the second is like unto it, Thou shalt love thy neighbour as thyself. On these two commandments hang all the law and the prophets" (Matt 22:37-39). In other words, at the heart of God's commandments is the divine call to love rightly.

So how does Beauty fit into shaping our loves in accordance with God's economy of goods?

One of the ways I like to illustrate how Beauty fits into this is with the Greek mythology of the Muses and the Sirens: The Muses are the daughters of Zeus who inspire Beauty and Truth, while the Sirens are water nymphs that lure sailors to their death through their bewitching songs. Both involve what appears to be Beauty, but with very different outcomes: one leads to life, while the other leads to death. The key to the difference is found in discerning what such attraction evokes in our souls: Beauty awakens a desire to surrender oneself to the object of attraction, whereas false beauty awakens a desire to control and dominate the object of attraction. Beauty awakens love; false beauty elicits lust. Truth attracts, lies seduce.

I once heard an excellent lecture on a theology of sexuality by a scholar who's also a Catholic nun, and she asked the audience: What does a prostitute get paid for? And the audience chuckled and didn't know what to say, particularly to a nun! Do you know how she answered her own question? *A prostitute gets paid to leave.* The prostitute does not get paid for the sex; the prostitute gets paid to leave after the lustful encounter. Love surrenders itself to the object of its attraction; lust dominates and controls it.

The Christian apologist Ravi Zacharias tells the story of a trial in which a lawyer was defending a publisher of pornography against anti-smut laws. The lawyer of this pornographer put one of the plaintiffs on the stand and began to ask: "Sir, have you ever gone into an art gallery?" The plaintiff of course said, "Yes." The lawyer then asked: "Sir, have you ever paid to go into an art gallery?" The plaintiff again said, "Yes." The lawyer then asks: "Sir, were there paintings of naked women in that art gallery?" The plaintiff then said: "Yes." The lawyer turns to the jury and says, "Sir, would you please explain to the ladies and gentlemen of this jury why it is that when you pay to see naked women, it's art, but when my client's clientele pays to see naked women, it's pornography? Can you please explain that to us?"

Now, dare I say, this lawyer is what the ancient wisdom tradition would have called a moral zombie. He's an illiterate imbecile when it comes to the very important distinction between love and lust. The simple, straightforward answer to his moronic inquiry is that one form of nudity awakens my loves while the other form awakens my lusts; one rightly orients us towards the True, Good, and Beautiful while the other orients us towards dehumanizing control and domination. One is aligned with God's economy of goods while the other rejects the existence of such a divine economy, reducing everything of value to a matter of mere subjective taste and personal preference. One attracts, the other seduces.

So, when our students are attracted to something they find beautiful, we have to teach them to discern *what* it is they are being attracted to by asking: Is it True and Good? For example, Lady Gaga music videos may attract me, but they do so in drawing me to something, namely, a world devoid of meaning and purpose that is there to be conformed to my needs and desires. This is why she is always at the center of the screen in her videos. Her artistry celebrates the emancipation of the sovereign self.

Of course, this is not to say that there is *nothing* True or Good about Lady Gaga's music. She is, after all, situated within 2,500 years of a musical tradition that was preserved and perfected by the church. It is to say, however, that the student needs to develop discernment when listening to her music so as to be able to approve of the Good and reject the lies.

So, the first thing we need to get is this: Beauty is a physics; it's a gravitational pull that draws me to the True and the Good. And secondly, it draws me to the True and Good by awakening within me a self-emptying love that seeks to serve the object of my affections rather than control and dominate it.

So how do we effectively teach this to our students? How do we awaken them to the True, the Good, and the Beautiful in a life transformative way that shapes their loves and desires with God's economy of goods?

CHAPTER 3

Redeeming the Senses

I argued above that in our pursuit of Truth, Goodness, and Beauty, we as classical educators can all too often fall short of such pursuits by adopting inadvertently modern conceptions of life in our pedagogies. For example, when I first taught an Aesthetics course at my university, I spent the entire semester reading and lecturing on texts with my students. It was basically a history of ideas course. I was teaching students the *facts* about the history of art and beauty. My pedagogy revealed a vision of education that was essentially *informative* rather than *formative*. I was teaching my students that competency and expertise in facts and information – the very values of our modern industrial age – were normative and desirable.

What I missed was rather simple yet quite profound: Art and beauty are not merely *what* we know, they are *how* we know. Beauty is not merely the object of our knowledge, beauty *is* knowledge.

It is here that I want to introduce the Christian tradition I refer to as the *redemption of the senses*. Briefly, the redemption of the senses involves a re-directing or re-training of the senses away from the carnal and the sensual and toward the eternally True, Good, and Beautiful. Christians believed that it was not just our souls that fell with the first sin in the garden, but our bodily senses became disordered as well. Thus, in the context of Christ's redemption of the world, the purpose of music and the arts was to sanctify our senses in such a way that our bodies become prepared for their future resurrection when Christ returns.

In accordance with the notion of Beauty as a law of attraction that draws our loves to the True and Good, we need to teach our students that the whole purpose of music and the arts is to provide an aesthetic bridge that facilitates a communion between the human soul and the True, the Good, and the Beautiful. This mediation is what makes art *good* art, or music *good* music; music and art are good if they fulfill their purpose, which is to serve as mediators between the loves of the human person and that eternal reality which the human person ought to love, and thereby cultivate virtue, which the classical tradition defines as rightly ordered loves.

So good art and music – as mediators of this communion – anticipate and prepare us for the transfiguration of the cosmos when Christ returns by giving us a foretaste of that transfiguration in the present. When your students get that, watch out! You're not going to be able to even remotely contain their enthusiasm, their love for good art and music explodes!

In what follows in Part II, we will explore this conceptual understanding of Beauty and the redeeming of the senses as it applies to school culture. How can we go about beautifying our schools to make them sacred spaces for the contemplation and encounter of the True, the Good, and the Beautiful, cultivating the affections of our students to love what's truly lovely and desire what's truly desirable and hence experience human flourishing?

Part II

CREATING A HIGH AESTHETIC IN OUR SCHOOLS

CHAPTER 4

Music

I think one of the great impoverishments in our schools is that the musical means of learning tends to die out after sixth or seventh grade. Chants fill the classrooms in the grammar school, only to be eclipsed by the lectern in the upper school, and we sequester singing to the specialization of the choir teacher.

At Tall Oaks Classical School, we emphasize filling our school building with music. Ideally, music is sonically seeping out of our windows and the cracks of our doors; it is rare to walk up and down hallways of K-12 classrooms and not hear somewhere in your short journey singing from some classroom.

What we do in the upper school is we have the students sing from the psalter at the beginning of class, in four-part harmony, as a way of sanctifying the space before the lesson begins. It's common of course to offer a prayer at the beginning of class, and that's great; but it was Augustine who rightly said, "He who sings, prays twice."

We have to understand that for the ancients, music was not understood as something performed, composed, practiced, or played; rather music was a mathematics, and mathematics involved the patterns of perfection upon which the entire cosmos was modeled. And while you can't see numbers, you can hear them through the frequencies of tones and the ratios of intervallic relationships (octaves, thirds, fifths).

Our students, by learning to sing, learn how to live in a harmonious relationship with the cosmos redeemed in Christ. We've been doing this for years at Tall Oaks, and I am convinced that they learn more theology from singing than from any lecture I can give. And I can honestly tell you, nothing has contributed to the formation of distinctively Christian culture in our upper school than getting our students to sing throughout the school day.

There are basically five ways to incorporate music throughout the school day:

1. Allocate certain times in the day for plenary singing and prayer. We sing together as an entire upper school first thing in the morning, along with reciting corporate prayer. Students also sing together the Doxology at lunch, and sometimes at the end of the school day.

2. Organize music according to the seasons. We program the music and prayers in the morning according to the liturgical calendar (Advent, Christmas, Epiphany, Lent, and Easter). This gives students a sense of the rhythm of sacred time.

3. Use music in Latin and Greek class. This is a wonderful opportunity for students to learn Gregorian Chant and the Greek Octoechos, the eight tones, each representing a different spiritual state. There are a number of resources on the web where you can print out musical notation for Latin and Greek chants.

4. Begin class with singing. I just eluded to this. Many classes at Christian schools begin with prayer. But I am not at all exaggerating when I say that as an educator, perhaps the most important parts of the school day are the times at the beginning of class when we sing psalms. This is because singing entails the power to create sacred space, a sanctified environment that can in turn sanctify all that goes on subsequently in the classroom. Singing harmonizes not merely the environment of the student, but the students themselves, bringing them in harmony with one another (you can't fight while you're singing together) and with themselves.

If you are unfamiliar with a psalter, I would suggest *The Book of Psalms for Worship* published by Crown & Covenant and the psalter-hymnal, *Cantus Christi,* published by Canon Press.

5. Learn to sing in parts. Unison singing is fine (especially in the context of ancient chant). But singing in parts helps the students to understand themselves as embodying the unity in diversity in the fellowship of the Trinity. It also opens up to them a whole new world of historic psalm and hymn singing.

There are a number of resources that teach part singing as well, such as the Vanguard System (http://singinparts.com/). And if you don't read music, you need look no further than YouTube for a number of video instructionals on learning musical notation.

Note that my students are not learning to sing psalms in music class; they learn it in theology class. Why? Because this *is* theology; theology in its richest expression. These are creatures living in harmony with a creation that is the artistic expression of the eternal artist.

By incorporating music throughout the school day, not only will you cultivate the senses and foster the virtues of your students, but you will develop community and comradery among students and teachers, awaken the beauty of Christian culture, and enhance the beauty of the school environment. I can't think of a more wonderful practice.

CHAPTER 5

Art

Along with cultivating a distinctively Christian acoustic environment in our schools, we ought to be concerned with the sanctification of the visual as well. Now, our school, as well as a number of schools I've had the privilege of visiting, have begun to stress the importance of pictorial imagery for cultivating the visual imagination of students. I know of some schools that have parents who are artists, and because either they own their school building or they've gotten permission from the church or building renter, they've painted murals in hallways or very lovely wall paintings in classrooms.

Here, when it comes to artwork, I believe it's important for students to learn how to 'read' an artwork, and this involves fostering the practice of what is called *gazing*, a practice employed by 'reading' iconography. The visual arts provide the opportunity to sanctify sight by uniting our eyes with our intellect, such that the depiction of divine images is experienced by both sight and soul. By learning to gaze at a piece of art, we train our students to begin to see the created order around them as itself a grand cosmic artwork.

One example I like to use with my students is the painting *Ecce Ancilla Domini* by the nineteenth-century English artist Gabriel Rossetti.[1]

You'll notice in this painting a number of striking features: the use of white for both Mary and Gabriel, the blue backdrop, and the red loom colored in red adorned with lilies complimenting the lily held in the hands of Gabriel. Make sure your students know the meanings behind the classical color schemes: blue signifies eternity, red signifies love, white represents purity, green signifies life, gold represents the presence of God, black signifies death to oneself. Lead the students to explore the meaning of the painting as the colors come together to tell a story. For example, the red loom in the front right with white lilies could signify the blood of Christ through which paradise is restored. The lily is also historically associated with the Virgin Mary.

Note, too, the dove between Gabriel and Mary? What is the significance of the dove in Scripture? Of course, the Holy

---

[1] You can access a full color depiction here:
http://www.rossettiarchive.org/docs/s44.rap.html.

Spirit. Does the dove take on any new significance against the backdrop of the blue garment? Perhaps an echo of Christ's baptism or Noah?

But notice further Mary's countenance; why does she appear so concerned? Invite the students to reflect on this; it's actually my opening question prompt to get the discussion going. Then, finally, show them the shape made by Gabriel's left hand as it intersects with the lily in his other hand: we see the sign of the cross. Mary's eyes are staring at a symbol that is teaching her that not only is she going to give birth to the Messiah, but he will be the sacrificial Lamb of God taking away the sins of the world.

When you teach your students how to read a painting, and then fill your classroom and hallways with beautiful art work prints, the students will sit in front of a painting for hours gazing, sanctifying their sight by uniting their eyes with their intellect.

CHAPTER 6

Spatial Arrangements

Our buildings, hallways, and classrooms are profoundly important when it comes to contemplating the True, Good, and Beautiful. The space surrounding our students constitutes what scholar Peter McLaren calls the 'hidden curriculum' within our schools; the subtle messages that are sent to our students through our day to day practices, particularly in terms of spatial arrangements and interior design.

You see the artwork on the walls, a number of library shelves with books, and notice that there's no desks in my room except for mine in the corner. Instead of individual desks, I have several tables that form a long three-sided rectangle with a number of comfortable fold-up chairs, along with a table in the middle, which is situated over a Persian rug, and with my lectern in front.

Now, when you walk in, you obviously know this is a place of learning; this is not a locker room; it's not a faculty lounge; it's a place of learning: The lectern facing one way, the chairs facing the other way, the books on the shelf giving an overall library feel. This is a place of learning. This is an example of what McLaren calls the 'hidden curriculum' within our schools. We need to be very cognizant of our hidden curriculum when it comes to our classroom arrangements so as to awaken and order our students loves.

Now, interior design often begins with a focal point in the room; in church architecture, this is historically the altar, the origin or source of communion. The rest of the church historically speaking harmonized with the altar. Similarly, in our classrooms, we have our own altar, as it were: Our classrooms tend to center on a rectangular object, namely the whiteboard or chalkboard.

Notice the four corners here; four is a cosmic number in the classical imagination. Four represents the elements of the cosmos (earth, air, fire, and water), the four directions (north, south, east, west), the four constituents of three-dimensional space (point, line, plane, solid), the four rivers in the Garden of Eden, and, of course, the Four Gospels. Thus, in a sense, this is our altar, and the lectern is our pulpit. We are teaching eternity as it is framed by these cosmic dimensions! So, this is our focal point.

I have Rublev's Trinity icon above, so this is the communion of which the whiteboard is itself an extension. The Trinity is revealed in the world through the Four Gospels, an icon of each situated in the four corners of the white board. And here too, I see an icon of classical education: The Trivium (grammar, dialectic, rhetoric) above (represented by the Trinity) is united with the Quadrivium (arithmetic, geometry, music, astronomy) below (represented by the white board); in the front of my classroom, the Word becomes flesh.

The lectern is then an extension of the whiteboard, working in harmony with the world revealed on the board. My words are being understood as an extension of this grand cosmic communion to which we are called.

The rest of the room would then in effect frame the whiteboard, creating a threshold, setting it apart, while at the same time growing out of it. This is what the scholar of sacred space Duncan G. Stroik would call the 'centripetal force' of the whiteboard: it draws us to itself, and at the same time it imparts sacredness to the areas surrounding it.

Note, too, that around the rug, I have tables rather than desks. I like tables, because tables suggest conversation. What do you do around tables? In the Rhetoric Stage, as it were, I want my students talking and talking a lot, I want a lot of *conversio*.

Notice further the difference for the student. What does a classroom set up with individual desks in fixed rows convey? Well it certainly may convey the idea that learning is a solitary activity undertaken by a sovereign individual irrespective of any other student in the classroom. After all, it's my report card, isn't it? But what do tables do, with several students sitting at the same table? It creates a sense of community.

So here I just want to inspire you to think of your classrooms as revelatory of a 'hidden curriculum,' messages that are communicated through spatial arrangement and interior design. At the very least, we need to transform our classrooms into sacred spaces, that is, spaces wherein the students know they are going to encounter the True, the Good, and the Beautiful in a life transforming way. That of course means that our rooms have to be arranged according to their particular subject; music rooms should have good acoustics; science labs need to have higher tables; a gymnasium requires open space and high ceilings. Regardless, students should be able to discern the beauty of the room, a space wherein they are going to encounter something that is life-transformative.

CHAPTER 7

Gardens and Landscaping

A number of schools are taking seriously the beautification of their school grounds. Of course, landscaping and gardening will be governed by your facilities, especially if you are renting. But it's hard to believe that owners of a property would not want that property beautified. This task is often undertaken by parent-volunteers; but if your school has a budget for this, it is well worth raising and spending the money for.

To better appreciate the role of gardens in the Christian life, I couldn't recommend more highly the little book, *The Fragrance of God*, by Vigen Guroian. Guroian beautifully illustrates the importance of gardens as foretastes of new creation. He shares how early Christians envisioned the Person of Christ as nothing less than the return of Paradise. This is particularly evident in the Greek and Syrian traditions, where Christ is seen as the Logos, the One through whom all things were made, who was originally revealed in his acts of creation, particularly in the habitat of Paradise. But as a result of our fall and the cursing of creation, we lost Paradise; so the

Logos becomes man in order to reveal to us once again the Paradise of God's presence in our midst.

One of the most beautiful gifts that we can give to our students is the realization that Jesus *is* Paradise; his cross is the Tree of Life; the waters of Eden are restored in the waters of baptism; the grain and fruit of the third day of creation are transformed into the bread and wine identified with the body and blood of Christ, such that creation and incarnation come together to restore our relationship with God and one another and hence perpetuate the life of the world. It is these Edenic frames of reference that inform the church's contemplation of a distinctively Christian vision of Truth, Goodness, and Beauty.

This is why I take my students every year to Longwood Gardens, a thousand-plus acres of gardens and meadows in Kennett Square, Pennsylvania, just a thirty-minute drive from our school. I want students to experience the redemption of their senses in an environment akin to our original garden paradise that is restored in Christ.

We also have an outdoor classroom, which is a picturesque setting with benches and a lectern to conduct class outside in the beauty of God's creation.

I want to draw your attention as well to Chris Hall of Covenant School in Charlottesville, VA, who's doing wonderful work in incorporating gardens into the scientific curriculum so as to awaken the student's love for creation as a prerequisite for the scientific study of creation. In fact, in one of his presentations, he puts up on a PowerPoint screen a contrast of two pictures of different scientific laboratories. On the one side, we see a picture of your typical sterile scientific lab room:

On the other side, we see a picture of a lush beautiful Edenic garden:

Chris then asks: Which scientific laboratory would we rather be in? Which one is more beautiful? And so what Chris does is he starts students in the grammar stage studying science in and through a garden, so as to awaken their love for creation before they go into the lab and study the natural world in far more micro detail.

If we take seriously gardens and the landscaping surrounding our schools, we'll find that our students cultivate a renewed sense of the master Gardener and the return of Paradise in Christ.

CHAPTER 8

School Culture

Thus far, we've focused on various components that constitute the formal arts, such as music, art, interior design, and horticulture. Classically conceived, the arts were considered mediators of divine meaning that shaped our loves in accordance with the divine economy of goods. However, aesthetic theory is not limited to the arts proper; it can be applied to school culture and curriculum as well, for as with the notion of the hidden curriculum we explored above, both function as mediators as well. In this chapter, we'll look at the ways in which school culture can communicate Beauty, and in the next chapter, we'll explore the various ways in which school curriculum can serve as an aesthetic mediator.

The way we approach our school community and culture is very much relevant to the notion of Beauty in the lives of our students. Like a flower garden, a Christocentric life needs to be cultivated in a particular kind of space in order to grow and blossom.

I think the school, first and foremost, must be appreciated as a place constituting a sacred space for the contemplation and practice of the True, Good, and Beautiful in the lives of our students so as to allow their faith to flourish. I think it foundational that we lead our students into appreciating that the various practices, arrangements, standards, and etiquettes that make up the life of the school collectively reveal the school as sacred space, a place sanctified, set apart from the world as a lived-out expression of a people in but not of the world.

I don't need to tell you this; you're going to get challenged by student and parent alike on precisely why you have the rules and standards of your school; you're going to eventually get some push back. And if you respond with: "Well that's just the way we do it," or "We have uniforms because we don't want anyone wearing anything inappropriate," the student or parent is going to smell a rat. They're going to recognize that the school's rules and standards are basically arbitrary; they're just there because someone has the power to put them there.

However, when you explain that the rules, etiquettes, and standards of the school are *revelatory* of Beauty, I've found that you will often get an entirely different response. By understanding the school as sacred space, students and parents immediately realize something: *Sacred spaces require special rules.* That's what sets December 25th apart from any other day; for that day to be special, we do special things that ordinarily would seem out of place. Special places require special rules.

And we need to underscore that the whole purpose of these rules and standards is not to stifle or impede, but rather to awaken and free; as G.K. Chesterton wrote in his *Orthodoxy*: "The more I considered Christianity, the more I found that while it had established a rule and order, the chief aim of that order was to give room for good things to run wild."

Just like in sports or music, the magic only begins to happen when one learns, masters, and indeed loves the rules.

Take, for example, school uniforms. Why do we require uniforms in our school? School uniforms demonstrate a common *telos*, that is, a common purpose or goal. This is the case with *all* uniforms – whether in sports or military or the clergy – all uniforms embody a *shared* identity, a *shared* purpose, and thus our students are encouraged to exercise their individual gifts for the benefit of the whole group, the whole community, to the glory of God. Hence, Paul could write to the Galatians: "All of you who have been baptized in Christ have been *clothed* with Christ ... we are all *one* in Christ" (Gal 3:27-28).

And that shared purpose or goal is itself found in the color of the uniforms. As we noted above, colors have significance in Christian theology: gold represents the presence of God, red reveals love, white purity, black death to self, green newness of life. Our uniforms at Tall Oaks are blue, which represents eternity. I love reminding our students that every time they put on that uniform, they are being prepared for eternity.

When the issue of school standards are questioned, look into the eyes of your students and say: By embodying these special rules, they reveal that you yourself are sacred; you've been set apart; you've been bought at a price.

CHAPTER 9

Curriculum

There are a number of ways to reimagine your course subjects and curriculum as revelatory of Beauty. First and foremost, I think we need to think of each one of our subjects as a mediator, an instrumental portal by which we encounter a vision of Christ unique to that subject. That means that I get a vision of Christ that is unique to Literature, to History, Art, Music, Science, Math or Gym. Every subject provides its own unique glimpse of the glory and majesty of Christ.

To help us better conceive of that, we can think of our courses as metaphors. For example, when a lover hands his betrothed a rose, what is going on there? Does the lover believe that his betrothed has an affinity for botany? Of course not. The rose is presented not *merely* as a rose or as a plant, but rather as a tangible expression, a concrete manifestation, of the person's love. The rose represents, literally *re*-presents, substantially something that otherwise would have been abstract and impalpable, namely, 'love.'

In this sense, the metaphor is a new set of eyes through which we see something we otherwise could not see. A metaphor awakens intangible spiritual realities to our senses, enabling us to encounter those realities in a life-transformative way.

Here's a sampling of how your curriculum can serve as a mediator between the student and the True, the Good, and the Beautiful and thereby cultivate the students' affections.[2]

Now, in terms of our school subjects functioning as metaphor, this of course has direct parallels with the world of literature. We 'see' through stories when we see that they point beyond themselves to a larger story, they are microcosms of a larger narrative macrocosm. Whether we are dealing with children's literature or Shakespeare, stories give us a taste of the meaning of our world through the narrative world. Thus, Shakespeare's tragedies are seen to represent the fall of humanity and his comedies represent our redemption; *Sleeping Beauty* can be seen as a story about a Christ-redeemer who slays the dragon and rescues his betrothed, by raising her to life. In *Pinocchio*, the hardened wood represents laziness, lying, and self-centeredness, and his transformation into a human represents the divine processes of regeneration and transfiguration. The *Little Mermaid* represents the quest for eternal life; *Charlotte's Web* represents life as communion and friendship.

Along with opening up the student to life through the world of literature, we awaken the students' imagination through the metaphors of mathematics. The Greeks, following the Pythagorean school of thought, noticed that numbers don't exist in time and space. No one has ever seen the number '1' for example, none of us have bumped into the number '1,' no

---

[2] I've written more extensively on this in my book, *Awakening Wonder: A Classical Guide to Truth, Goodness, and Beauty* (Classical Academic Press, Camp Hill: PA, 2015).

one has heard, smelled it, etc. This is because the number '1' does not extend in time and space; it appears only as an adjective: one pencil, one book, one student. But the Greeks asked, what would happen to human civilization if we said that numbers and mathematics don't actually exist? We couldn't build bridges, or buildings, or roads, or anything; the regularity of the universe would be called into question; everything would collapse. So, our existence, our experience of numbers is testimony to the fact that numbers and mathematics must exist, *but they must exist in another world.* And because mathematics deals with a perfect and eternal world, then it must be a divine world. Mathematics represents, literally *re*presents, that divine world in this one, and thus every time I do mathematics, I am communing with divine life, or in Augustine's refinement, the architecture of a divine mind. You see, numbers aren't just numbers. They point beyond themselves to something that awakens awe and wonder within us. We begin to discover *meaning* through numbers.

Science can be seen as exemplative of Beauty as well. In fact, the medievals understood science very much as a species of aesthetics, the study of art and beauty. Medieval scholars assigned two attributes to Beauty: What we might call an aesthetics of proportion (which is the *quantitative* nature of Beauty) and an aesthetics of light or luminosity (which is the *qualitative* nature of Beauty). An aesthetics of proportion involved the idea of 'congruence' (*congruentia*), balance, consonance, harmony. This is the *quantity* of medieval aesthetics. But by the thirteenth century, light and luminosity became the central *quality* of medieval aesthetics. The thirteenth-century bishop Robert Grossetest (cf. 1245) wrote: "Light is truly the principle of all beauty; light, as the principle of color, is the beauty and ornament of all that is visible." And it is these quantitative and qualitative conceptions of Beauty that extended out into the observable world of medieval science. For example, luminosity was itself the outgrowth of scientific developments in the field of optics. Medieval theologians, philosophers, scientists, poets, architects were fascinated by optics, colors, rainbows, mirrors, and prisms. Indeed, the Latin term for Beauty, *pulcher*, seems to be etymologically derived from the Greek *poly-chroia* or 'many-colored.'

Science and Beauty, along with geometry, came together in many ways most explicitly in the sacred space of the medieval cathedral. The circular dome represented heaven, with the circle representing eternity, the four corners of the floor represent the four corners of the earth, particularly Byzantine churches were a perfect square, representing the Holy of Holies, often there were four pillars that stretched down from the heavenly dome to the earthly floor which represented the four gospels testifying that heaven has come down to earth in Christ. And of course, the cruciform became the standard floor plan in the Christian west so that every church was a tangible representation of the world recreated through the cross.

In classical education, physical education or *gymnastikē* is particularly important for mediating Beauty to our students. Athletics in the classical world were inextricably linked to the virtue of self-mastery or self-control, (*engkratia*), the formation of an excellent disposition, which was the key virtue that separated the Greek from the Barbarian. Thus, the language of athletic competition was often used to think about the development of the virtue of self-mastery in the life of a philosopher. We see Paul appealing to athletic imagery in 1 Cor 9:24-26 as a metaphor for his mastery over passions and temptations in the context of forgoing his legitimate prerogatives as an apostle for the sake of serving others in the gospel. So athletic competition can be this wonderful embodiment of the Christian life, where one masters a set of rules for the sake of others so that good things run wild.

So literature, math, science, gym, as well as music and the arts, are all revelatory in their own unique ways of a world filled with Truth, Goodness, and Beauty. Thus, by seeing through our subjects as metaphoric mediators, our subject matter transforms into a new set of eyes through which our students can begin to see the meaning inherent in our created order.

SUMMARY

The goal of this book was to provide a primer on Beauty to cultivate a high aesthetic in our schools. My own experience in the world of classical education corroborates the need for such a primer. As educators focused on shaping the worldview of our students, we often focus on Truth and Goodness at the expense of Beauty. When it comes to overlooking the importance of aesthetics in the cultivation of the loves of our students, I have been the chief of sinners. This book is part of my ongoing repentance.

First, we learned that Beauty is a physics, a gravitational pull that draws us to the True and the Good, and it does so by awakening and aligning our loves with God's economy of goods. Beauty thus enables us to love what God loves and desire what God desires. Through Beauty, we cultivate both wisdom (envisioning the world as filled with divine meaning and purpose) and virtue (ordering one's loves in accordance with that divine meaning and purpose) in the lives of our students.

Secondly, we rehearsed a number of ways in which we can transfigure our school community with the transformative power of Beauty. We looked at how music, art, spatial arrangements, gardens and landscaping, school culture, and curriculum can serve as mediators, as a collective aesthetic bridge that facilitates a communion between the souls of our students and the True, the Good, and the Beautiful.

The crucial takeaway from all this is that classical education is ultimately about the training of our students' affections to love what is truly lovely and desire what is truly desirable, and hence experience human flourishing. It is Beauty that more than anything cultivates the student's loves and affections. By implementing a high aesthetic into every facet of school life, we provide the conditions whereby the lives of our students can transform into paragons of wisdom and virtue, as they are drawn into the life of God's infinite Beauty.

Thank you again for purchasing this book!

I hope this book helped to awaken you to the nature of Beauty and the various ways in which Beauty can be incorporated into every facet of school life and culture.

If you enjoyed this book, then I'd like to ask you for a favor: Would you be kind enough to leave a review for this book on Amazon? I would so greatly appreciate it!

Thank you so much, and may God richly bless you!

Steve Turley

www.turleytalks.com

Check Out My Other Books

Below you'll find some of my other popular books that are popular on Amazon. Simply go to the links below to check them out. Alternatively, you can visit my author page on Amazon to see my other works.

- *Classical vs. Modern Education: A Vision from C.S. Lewis* http://amzn.to/2opDZju

- *Ever After: How to Overcome Cynical Students with the Role of Wonder in Education* http://amzn.to/2jbJI78

- *Movies and the Moral Imagination: Finding Paradise in Films* http://amzn.to/2zjghJj

- *Health Care Sharing Ministries: How Christians are Revolutionizing Medical Cost and Care* http://amzn.to/2B2Q8B2

- *The Face of Infinite of Love: Athanasius on the Incarnation* http://amzn.to/2oxULNM

- *President Trump and Our Post-Secular Future: How the 2016 Election Signals the Dawning of a Conservative Nationalist Age* http://amzn.to/2B87Q22

- *Stressed Out: Learn How an Ancient Christian Practice Can Relieve Stress and Overcome Anxiety* http://amzn.to/2kFzcpc

- *Wise Choice: Six Steps to Godly Decision Making*
  http://amzn.to/2qy3C2Z

- *Awakening Wonder: A Classical Guide to Truth, Goodness, and Beauty* http://amzn.to/2ziKR5H

- *Worldview Guide for* A Christmas Carol
  http://amzn.to/2BCcKHO

- *The Ritualized Revelation of the Messianic Age: Washings and Meals in Galatians and 1 Corinthians*
  http://amzn.to/2B0mGvf

If the links do not work, for whatever reason, you can simply search for these titles on the Amazon website to find them.

About www.TurleyTalks.com

Are we seeing the revitalization of Christian civilization?

For decades, the world has been dominated by a process known as globalization, an economic and political system that hollows out and erodes a culture's traditions, customs, and religions, all the while conditioning populations to rely on the expertise of a tiny class of technocrats for every aspect of their social and economic lives.

Until now.

All over the world, there's been a massive blowback against the anti-cultural processes of globalization and its secular aristocracy. From Russia to Europe and now in the U.S., citizens are rising up and reasserting their religion, culture, and nation as mechanisms of resistance against the dehumanizing tendencies of secularism and globalism.

And it's just the beginning.

The secular world is at its brink, and a new traditionalist age is rising.

Join me each week as we examine these worldwide trends, discover answers to today's toughest challenges, and together learn to live in the present in light of even better things to come.

So hop on over to www.TurleyTalks.com and have a look around. Make sure to sign-up for our weekly Email Newsletter where you'll get lots of free giveaways, private Q&As, and tons of great content. Check out our YouTube channel (www.youtube.com/c/DrSteveTurley) where you'll understand current events in light of conservative trends to help you flourish in your personal and professional life. And of course, 'Like' us on Facebook and follow us on Twitter.

Thank you so much for your support and for your part in this cultural renewal.

About the Author

Steve Turley (PhD, Durham University) is an internationally recognized scholar, speaker, and classical guitarist. He is the author of *Awakening Wonder: A Classical Guide to Truth, Goodness, and Beauty* (Classical Academic Press) and *The Ritualized Revelation of the Messianic Age: Washings and Meals in Galatians and 1 Corinthians* (T&T Clark). Steve blogs on the church, society and culture, education, and the arts at TurleyTalks.com. He is a faculty member at Tall Oaks Classical School in Bear, DE, where he teaches Theology, Greek, and Rhetoric, and Professor of Fine Arts at Eastern University. Steve lectures at universities, conferences, and churches throughout the U.S. and abroad. His research and writings have appeared in such journals as *Christianity and Literature, Calvin Theological Journal, First Things*, *Touchstone*, and *The Chesterton Review*. He and his wife, Akiko, have four children and live in Newark, DE, where they together enjoy fishing, gardening, and watching *Duck Dynasty* marathons.

Made in the USA
Monee, IL
22 May 2023

34259221R00037